The boy who cried wolf

Story written by Alison Hawes
Illustrated by Tim Archbold

Speed Sounds

Consonants

Ask your child to say the sounds (not the letter names) clearly and quickly, in and out of order. Make sure he or she does not add 'uh' to the end of the sounds, e.g. 'f' not 'fuh'.

Each box contains one sound. Focus sounds for this story are circled.

f	l	m	n	r	s	v	z	sh	th	ng
ff	ll	mm	nn	rr	ss	ve	zz			nk
ph	le	mb	kn	wr	se		**se**			
			gn		**c**		s			
					ce					

b	c	d	g	h	j	p	qu	t	w	x	y	ch
bb	k	dd	gg		g	pp		tt	**wh**			tch
	ck		gu		ge							
					dge							

Vowels

Ask your child to say the sounds in and out of order.

a	e ea	i	o	u	ay a-e a	ee ea y e	igh i-e ie i	ow o-e o oe
at	h**e**n	**i**n	**o**n	**u**p	d**ay**	s**ee**	h**igh**	bl**ow**

oo u-e ue	oo	ar	or oor ore aw	air are	ir ur er	ou ow	oy oi
z**oo**	l**oo**k	c**ar**	f**or**	f**air**	wh**ir**l	sh**ou**t	b**oy**

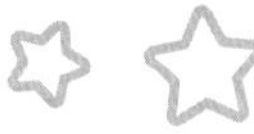

Story Green Words

For each word ask your child to read the separate sounds, e.g. 'b-u-s', 'p-oo-l' and then blend sounds together to make the word, e.g. 'bus', 'pool'. Sometimes one sound is represented by more than one letter, e.g. 'th', 'oo'. These are underlined.

flock noise each safe lie cried wolf*

Ask your child to say the syllables and then read the whole word.

Iss|am hun|gry vill|age a|sleep sulk|il|y nev|er

Ask your child to read the root first and then the whole word with the suffix.

live → lived dream → dreaming sudden → suddenly

trick → tricks attack → attacking trust → trusted

place → places plea → pleas ignore → ignored

* *Challenge Words*

Vocabulary Check

Tell your child the meaning of each word in the context of the story.

	definition:	**sentence:**
live up to	*be as good as*	*"We trust you to live up to your name," said his mother.*
flock	*a group of sheep*	*Each day, Issam took the flock of sheep up to the hills...*
dull	*boring*	*Keeping the sheep safe was important, but Issam found it dull.*
pleas	*calls*	*But the people ignored his pleas for help.*
wept	*cried*	*"The flock is lost," he wept.*

Red Words

Red words don't sound like they look. Ask your child to read the words but if he or she gets stuck read the word to your child.

all	once	where	could
other	some	would	who
people	were	mother	over
why	now	through	what
there	any	one	old

The boy who cried wolf

Do not read the story to your child first. Point to the words as your child reads. If your child gets stuck on a word help him or her say the sounds and blend them together. Re-read each sentence to your child to help him or her remember what he or she has read. Discuss what is happening on each page.

Issam had an important job. He needed to keep all the sheep safe from the hungry wolf that lived in the hills.

"We trust you to live up to your name," said his mother. She never let him forget that his name meant 'to keep safe'.

Each day, Issam took the flock of sheep up into the hills to eat the sweet, green grass.

Keeping the sheep safe was important, but Issam found it dull. He lay in the grass dreaming of all the places he wished he could be. He wanted to have some *fun*!

One day, Issam was so bored he did something shocking. He stood at the top of the hill and cried out:

“Wolf! Wolf! A wolf is attacking the sheep! I need your help!”

The people from the village rushed up the hill to help Issam keep the flock safe. But when they reached him, there was no wolf to be seen.

"Issam – where is the wolf?" they shouted.
"There isn't one!" he mumbled.
"We trusted you," they cried. "What will your mother say?"

"Can't a boy have a bit of fun?" Issam said, sulkily.

The very next day he did the same thing.

“Wolf! Wolf!” he cried. “Please be quick or the wolf will eat the sheep!”

The people from the village rushed up the hill but, as before, there was no wolf. You have never seen people so angry! They shouted. They screamed. They yelled.

“No more tricks! We cannot trust you if you keep doing this.”

The next day, Issam was asleep beneath a leafy tree. Suddenly, the air was filled with the noise of bleating sheep.

Issam leapt to his feet.
"Oh no!" he screamed.
"It's a wolf!"

"Wolf! Wolf!" he cried, as loudly as he could.

But the people ignored his pleas for help.
"It's just one of Issam's tricks," they told each other.

"Help!" cried Issam. "There really *is* a wolf."
But nobody came. Nobody helped.
The wolf killed all the sheep.

Issam dragged his feet back to the village.
"The flock is lost," he wept. "Why didn't you help me?"

The people were very angry.
"You really do not know?" they shouted.
"Why do you think? We could not trust you. And now you have lost all our sheep."

Issam looked at the ground, red-faced.
From then on, he never told a lie.
But he became known as 'the boy who cried wolf'.

Now ask your child to re-read the story helping him or her think about the best way to read each sentence.

Questions to talk about

Read the questions aloud to your child and ask him or her to find the answers on the relevant pages. Do not ask your child to read the questions – the words are harder than he or she can read at the moment.

p.9 What was Issam's job?

p.10 Why did Issam pretend there was a wolf attacking the sheep?

p.11 Why did the people rush up the hill?

p.12 Why were the people from the village so angry?

p.14 Why do you think the people ignored Issam?

p.15 Issam said, "The flock is lost." What does this mean?

p.15 Issam looked at the ground, red-faced. What does this tell you about how he felt?

Questions to read and answer

Ask your child to read the questions and find the correct answer in the story.

1. Issam's name meant **to keep well / to keep healthy / to keep safe**.

2. Issam was **happy / bored / shocked** watching the sheep.

3. "A wolf is attacking the sheep!" cried **Issam's mother / the people / Issam**.

4. The people said they could not **trust / see / reach** Issam.

5. From then on, Issam never told a **tale / story / lie**.

Speedy Green Words

Ask your child to read the words clearly and quickly – across the rows, down the columns, and in and out of order.

help	need	name	say
day	angry	eat	sweet
really	hills	seen	boy
sheep	air	next	feet
our	live	tree	please